Michelle Pledger is a brilliant scholar and educator that has somehow managed to give us a text that offers equal parts theory, practice, inspiration, motivation and instruction. This is an absolute must read. I am thankful that it is out in the world.

-Dr. Christopher Emdin, Professor, University of Southern California, *Ratchedemic*

From the very opening of this pocket guide, Dr. Pledger connects with her audience in a high-energy way that makes teachers want to jump on board. The work in this guide is designed in a way that is easy to access for anyone — but especially for busy teachers. The checklists that are given throughout that provide the 'how' of the work are both helpful and practical, and they provide plenty of choices for teachers to approach the work in a way that makes sense to them. Dr. Pledger provides both theory and exercises for teachers to try, but additionally, she shows models and examples throughout to really allow educators to see the possibilities in reality. By the end of this reading, teachers will be able to identify pieces of the education system that might be hard to see while in the middle of them. It allows them to take a step back, analyze, and take action within their own schools, which is what will lead to true liberation for students.

-Tina Marie Schuster, Director of Pedagogy and Innovation, Center for Love and Justice,
Victims on Both Ends of the Gun

I deeply appreciate this book. There is an efficiency to the way that Michelle deals with complex ideas, like liberation, that is both uncommon and pitch perfect for this moment when educators are so worn down. The linked resources in the How? sections help add depth and nuance to the ideas while also opening up concrete paths to liberatory action. Most importantly, this book helps expand the reader's moral imagination by making it seem eminently doable to engage in the work of liberatory learning. In a moment where there is so much effort to quash historical truth-telling in service of liberation, these pages challenged and equipped me to make sure that liberation is not merely a rhetorical conviction, but a living practice.

-James May, Strategic Advisor, New Tech Network

The manner in which Dr. Pledger layers in each liberatory paradigm and skillfully presents each key resource honors not only our young people's experience and truth but the experience of the educators dedicated to the lifelong journey of liberation. The heart of the work beats true on every page.

-Dr. Andrea Frias, Director of Instructional Leadership and Development, High Tech High

Once in a while a meaningful and well-crafted book opens and challenges your mind. On rare occasions, a powerful text can touch your heart and in an even more rare moment a manuscript can reach deep into your soul. Dr. Pledger manages to do all three in Liberate! The prose, power, and practice contained within the text far exceeds any sized pocket and holds the power of deep and meaningful transformation.

-Dr. Alan J. Daly, Director of Educational Leadership Joint Doctoral Program, University of California, San Diego, *Social Network Theory and Educational Change*

Go ahead and get two because your copy will soon be highlighted, underlined, scribbled into, dog-eared, and tattered from constant use. Dr. Michelle Pledger pithily distills twenty years of her own teaching practice plus heaps of research and learning from her dissertation into a practical, tactical must-read guide for every Frierian educator committed to the discovery of true freedom.

-Becky Margiotta, Co-Founder of the Billions Institute, *Impact with Integrity: Repair the World without Breaking Yourself*

This book is what every educator needs to read! Dr. Pledger's excellent synthesis of anti-racist theory and pedagogy into a practical guide of liberatory classroom practices is transformative. Dr. Pledger shares practices of how to know your students deeply and create a culturally responsive learning environment, how to reflect and unpack our own biases that impact our students' daily lives, and how to liberate our curriculum and instruction. This is a courageous piece of work that has been missing amongst the great works of many anti-racist educators, researchers, and authors. This book demonstrates what liberation in schools can and should look like!

-Dr. Curtis Taylor, Center for Research on Equity and Innovation

This small book is a powerful gift to educators and schools from Michelle Pledger, who has curated a range of equity-centered resources to help us unleash the genius in all students from all backgrounds.

-Ron Berger, EL Education, *Leaders of Their Own Learning*

What an amazing gift Dr. Michelle Pledger is offering the world. Her authentic, loving, and challenging advice to adults on how they can support their own liberation while supporting liberatory learning for young people around them is so pragmatic, inspiring and powerful. This is not just a "must-read" for educators but for any leaders who are working to advance equity, joy and liberation. It is a powerful resource to turn to over and over again!

-Katie Hong, Nonprofit and Philanthropic Consultant and Coach, KH Consulting

Whether you're a novice teacher or a veteran, this book will transform your teaching forever! In this compelling pocket-sized guide, Dr. Pledger inspires us all to envision schools as a place of liberation and provides actionable insights for educators to make the changes necessary. Filled with resources and research that support educators to examine our beliefs and shift our practice, this book makes us all want to be better for our young people.

-Mari Jones, Director of Deeper Learning Hub

Liberate! is an overwhelmingly useful resource for practitioners, and for anyone who is wanting to live their lives and their relationships in revitalized and transformed community. Michelle's work is deeply researched and experienced, and has a laser-like focus on equity, coupled with practical ways to concretize practitioner's work. Most importantly, *Liberate!* is written with a deep sense of love - love of self, love of others, and love of what is possible in the world when our collective liberation is the focus.

-Michelle Molitor, Founder and Director of The Equity Lab

LIBERATE!
POCKET-SIZED PARADIGMS FOR LIBERATORY LEARNING

Michelle Sadrena Pledger
Foreword by Aisha Bain
Illustrated by CHIKLE

Living for Liberation

Copyright © 2022 Michelle Sadrena Pledger

All rights reserved. No part of this book may be reproduced or used in any manner without the prior written permission of the copyright owner, except for the use of brief quotations in a book review.

To request permissions, contact the author at info@livingforliberation.com

Paperback: 979-8-9855385-0-2

Library of Congress Number: 2022900794

First Paperback Edition: January 2022

Edited by Krista Galleberg
Cover art, illustrations, and layout by CHIKLE
Author photograph by Brent Spirnak

Printed in the USA.

Living for Liberation
PO Box 1745
Escondido, CA 92033

livingforliberation.com

Disclaimer: This book directs you to access third-party content via Web links, texts, videos, and podcasts recommendations. Living for Liberation makes no guarantee that third-party content will be available for your use and encourages you to review the terms and conditions of any third-party content you may encounter. Living for Liberation takes no responsibility and assumes no liability for your use of any third-party content, nor does Living for Liberation approve, sponsor, endorse, verify, or certify such third-party content.

To my mom and best friend,
Sadie Theresa Pledger.
You are forever free and resting in the arms
of our Heavenly Father.

And, to everyone who aspires to live for liberation.
Keep breathing, learning and loving.
It is possible within your lifetime.

Contents

Foreword	vii
Preface	xiii
Acknowledgements	xviii
I. Commencement	1
II. Liberate Your Consciousness!	7
III. Liberate Your Classroom!	15
IV. Liberate Your Curriculum!	23
V. Liberate Your Cognitive Capacity Bias!	33
VI. Liberate Your Communication!	41
VII. Liberate Your Conduct Constructs!	49
VIII. ~~Conclusion~~ Call to Action!	59
Appendix	62
References	70
Recommended Reading List	81
Contributor Biographies	83

Foreword

Your Fuel, Your Fire, Your Future You

We heard a plane in the distance, sucked in our breath, and listened with every cell in our body, praying that it would not turn this way and drop more bombs on the remains of this village scorched black and gray against the pale sands of the desert in Darfur, a war-torn region of Sudan. We got lucky and were spared, when so many people in Darfur were not. As we prepared to leave and share all that we had documented with the world, we asked each village what they needed, what they wanted the world to know. In every village, though they were displaced, living near the rubble of their homes, or under trees or makeshift housing of branches to shield themselves from the relentless Saharan sun - mothers, fathers, chiefs, elders, young people all said - schools. Please help us to support our children to learn and we will figure out the rest.

From Congo to California, one of the most enduring, unrelenting constants I have seen and been a part of, in more than twenty countries, has been the human devotion to learning. This global work brought Michelle Pledger and I together for the Deeper Learning Conference in 2021, and though COVID restricted us to Zoom - Michelle's energy, spirit, passion, and commitment to this work just reached through the screen and hugged my heart - and that was it - peoples for life!

I'm so excited for you to dive into this guide.

This pocket-sized powerhouse for liberatory learning supports beautiful, practical, and intentional ways you can decolonize learning and take specific actions towards liberated futures. As you dive into this realm of paradigms and possibility, I wanted to take a brief moment to remind you that each of us is the fuel for decolonization, and requires fuel to continue to decolonize ourselves, our learning communities, and to build our undeniable liberated futures.

Michelle's vision for what's possible for our young people, and for us all, fueled this guide at a time when she was experiencing deep hardship, and the entire world was trying to imagine a new year where 2022 did not translate to 2020 too. In all seriousness, this guide does not only ask of you, it gives to you, honoring that you need and deserve fuel, and that you are part of the fuel that makes liberatory learning possible - that makes liberation possible.

Following the flow of the guide, here's a little fuel - what, why, and how.

What?
I think of fuel in comparison to relationships in nature, as "nourishing, generative, sustaining, and interdependent." I couldn't find that definition anywhere, so I created my own because when the constructs around us don't support the liberation we need, we must create our own.

Why?

This work is for the long haul. The systems of oppression work from a scarcity model - there is not enough time in a day, there is not enough for all of us, thus move faster, work harder. Many of us know and experience the oppressive forces in our communities that attempt to crush our young people, especially those of color - and so we live and breathe the urgency we feel to change things as fast as possible.

It is true that our young people deserve immediate change. And "you are the fuel and you need fuel" is a reminder that white supremacy works optimally when the people who are trying to change it burn out, disconnect, and are forced to move so fast today that there is no time or energy to plan for the future. Moving too quickly ensures that the conditions around us restrict us to survival mode. Liberatory practices start and continue in you, and through you. How you choose to fuel yourself, how you choose to show up for yourself, and how you choose to model through your actions creates the liberatory conditions for you, for the young people you touch, and all those around you. Knowing what you need and deserve can help others claim the same.

How?

There are so many how's, I'm going to focus on two in particular, and you're invited to build upon and list more of your own.

- ☐ Envision! You might be looking at me funny right now, but this is one of the greatest sources of fuel you can have. Envision the future you want and need, dream about what learning communities can look like 100 years into the future - boundless from the realities and constructs of today. Oppression feeds you pre-configured futures within systems and structures that were not built for all of us in the first place. Visioning for the future breaks white supremacy's chains on our imaginations to see beyond what is to what can be, how you want to be a part of it, and how you can get there.
- ☐ Dream! Dream so big it feels daring and crazy - that means you're doing it right! Dreaming of things like young people in outdoor classrooms, with their hands in the dirt, where elders exchange learning sessions with young people, where young people rotate through learning modules and apprenticeships on solar energy hoverboards that allow them to connect to the things they love and all is equally valued in a community, where large pop-up screens in the sky connect young people from other countries - whatever you dream of not only becomes a nourishing north star for you, but a road map to ways to do that today. Such as having storytelling time with elders, bringing plants into the classrooms, etc. while working on structural changes that make these bigger changes possible long term.

What do young people dream about when they think of communities in the future? How can you vision and design together?

Identify what nourishes you, what is generative for you, and puh-lease put rest on that list!! I wish for you the most delicious, delightful, soulful, connective, generative, healing, and freeing forms of fuel, as you bring to life *Liberate! Pocket-Sized Paradigms for Liberatory Learning*.

Aisha Bain
Insurgent Imaginator
Chief Architect, Resistance Communications
Co-Founder Vision Not Victim
More receipts available on website:
https://www.resistancecommunications.com/

Preface

Dear Liberator,

When I grew up, San Bernardino, California was my zone of proximal development. My daily life traversed three distinct locations in that huge county. Garner Avenue was the Latinx barrio where we lived and where the "primas" down the street, Corrina and Grezel, were my first Spanish teachers. They taught me everyday words like "perro", "gato", "cama", and "bicicleta", as well as more mature words like "baboso" and "cochina". I even went so far as to affect a Spanish speaking accent when I spoke to them in English. The second location was Belvedere Elementary School. My mom used my aunt's address so that I could attend a "better" (and whiter) school that was out of our district. At Belvedere, I code-switched to "proper" English, sometimes using a borderline valley girl accent because I knew I did not resemble my peers, and I thought if I talked, laughed, and acted like them, they would somehow overlook my darker skin tone. With an absent father (he eventually came back) and an overworked mother, my brother and my after-school child care was transferred to my Auntie Ruth. She had four children of her own, so adding two more did not make much of a difference. At Auntie Ruth's house on Duffy Street, I often unsuccessfully tried to shift my speech to African American vernacular, aware that my cousins and the rest of the neighborhood kids attended the local schools nearby, not Belvedere. We performed rhythmic cheer routines on the Duffy street sidewalk, but I could never master double-dutch.

As a child my desire was to discover my place in the world, a place where I could feel a sense of unity. A sense of belonging. A sense of self. I struggled to find it. I was not Mexican enough for Garner Ave, not White enough for Belvedere, not Black enough for Duffy Street. To be honest, I lived in a perpetual state of discomfort in my own skin that lasted well into adulthood.

I did not always love myself because I did not know myself, and my schooling played a pivotal role in my controversial identity development. My schools were a place of whiteness. I spent Pre-K through 6th grade in predominantly White schools where I began to shed aspects of my cultural identity to obtain the prize of acceptance. The gravitational pull of assimilation was strong because I wanted to belong. I was praised for academic excellence in ways that implicitly communicated, *"you're different from those other black kids."* Truth be told, at the time it made me feel special, and I was oblivious to the hatred it engendered in me. Hatred for myself and my people. The cost of acceptance and achievement was cultural identity exclusion, and the internalized oppression I experienced during childhood, adolescence, and young adulthood took decades to dismantle. When I reflect on my education journey, my memories are tainted with a sense of shame when they could have been filled with a sense of belonging. I was never free.

The reality is many young people across our nation in public, private and charter schools still are not free. They spend a significant amount of time preparing for who not to be when they go to school-- how not to dress, behave, or speak. One can imagine how much mental energy is spent on verbal and behavioral self-monitoring—brain space that could be utilized for learning. Other young people go to school being their complete cultural selves only to be dismissed or disciplined for it. We in education love using terms like authentic audience and authentic assessments, but many of us still refuse to let students be their authentic selves. The liberation of young people is necessary, particularly when our students have had their lives disrupted by a deadly pandemic, their hope in humanity played with by politicians, and their belief in the justice system crushed by an officer's knee.

When I became a K12 educator, I endeavored to do things differently. During my fifteen year tenure in K12, I succeeded in some areas and failed in others, but I never stopped seeking growth, refinement, and freedom in my teaching. And as I work toward the liberation of myself and others in adult learning and professional development spaces, I am constantly thinking about how to reach more people to share what I have learned and what I am still learning.

This book has been percolating in my brain since the completion of my doctoral program in December of 2018. My dissertation,

"Cultivating Culturally Responsive Reform: The Intersectionality of Backgrounds and Beliefs on Culturally Responsive Teaching Behavior," focused on developing culturally responsive-sustaining teaching self-efficacy in novice and veteran teachers. When I opened a blank Google document on April 19th of 2020, I knew that I wanted whatever I was creating to be an accessible text with practical and powerful implications. I wanted it to be evidence-based and practitioner-based. And I wanted it to go beyond culturally responsive-sustaining pedagogy. I have taken the time to conduct research, read books and articles, watch panels, keynotes, and documentaries, observe classrooms, teach courses, and learn from authors, experts, K12 teachers, graduate school instructors, and most importantly, young people. The original title was *Not Today Colonizer! Pocket-Sized Protection from the Colonizer in Your Classroom*. The title was a hit! People laughed and lauded the pithy phrasing, but I changed my mind. I did not want to center the oppressor or only focus on what's problematic. I wanted to synergize with the liberator and foment what's possible. That is how *Liberate! Pocket-Sized Paradigms for Liberatory Learning* came into existence.

The content in this book is rooted in material and human resources, and in my twenty years of experience as an educator. The terminology, research, and best practices included in this book are a representation of my current knowledge, thinking, and understanding. I am keenly aware that terms evolve over time, as do research and best practices. I give myself permission to believe what I believe now, and the grace to refine my thinking in the future. That is the power and beauty of being a lifelong learner. Especially a liberated one.

I hope you ponder, practice, and proliferate any wisdom you may encounter in this text.

In love and liberation,

Michelle

P.S. I have an alliteration addiction that might annoy you. But in the words of Beyoncé, "I Ain't Sorry."

Acknowledgements

I want to express my deep appreciation and gratitude for the following beings (spiritual and physical):

God, for blessing me with the gift of teaching, learning, and an unyielding hope in humanity.

My ancestors for infusing their strength, wisdom, brilliance and resilience into my heart, mind, body and soul.

My parents, sweet Sadie and dear Dwight, for loving, challenging, and supporting me in one way or another throughout my entire lifetime.

Dr. Gloria Ladson-Billings, Dr. Lisa Delpit, Dr. Geneva Gay, Dr. Christoper Emdin, Dr. H. Samy Alim, Dr. Django Paris, Dr. Gholdy Muhammad, and Zaretta Hammond for your scholarly work and its impact on my education philosophy.

Aisha Bain for knowing and loving me enough to write a fierce foreword.

Krista Galleberg for thoughtful and meticulous editing, appendix, and reference list preparation.

CHIKLE for your beautiful cover art, in-text illustrations, book layout and unlimited encouragement.

Carlos Tirado and the Orange Glen Print Shop for quality printing of my first book baby.

Dr. Stacey Caillier and Dr. Diana Cornejo-Sanchez for your expert critique of my first draft which made this work stronger.

Dr. Curtis Taylor, Dr. Felicia Singleton, Tina Schuster and Mari Jones for your valuable feedback on specific sections.

My "man-friend" aka life partner, Domonique Crawford for your unwavering support of all my ambitions.

My dog (Black) Mamba for enduring my absence when I went to the coffee shop to write, and for sleeping right beside me when I wrote at home.

I love you all immensely. ♥

xx

I. COMMENCEMENT

I. Commencement
commencement: a beginning or start

I believe that most educators in most educational institutions want to do right by all young people. And the most anti-racist, culturally responsive, social justice driven educators want to advance opportunities, equity, and access for young people from historically marginalized communities. Yet we educators face competing commitments that monopolize our time, energy, and attention. Capacity building for any education initiative necessitates time, professional development, and coaching, but not all teachers have access to these resources, and definitely not in equal measure.

As a former high school teacher, I fully appreciate that teachers often lack the capacity to read heady education research books and theoretical articles. This pocket guide is a compendium of practical resources to support your efforts in cultivating a decolonized, and subsequently liberated classroom. It includes accessible approaches and resources to help you engage, sustain or deepen equitable practices in your classroom. Good news, I wrote this pocket-sized book in this way so that you will not be intimidated by the length, the academic language, or the need to wade through a ton of educational theory (though it is heavily grounded in theory and practice). And I made it pocket-sized so that you can easily carry it around with you in your backpacks, purses, fanny packs, or pockets.

Whether you are a novice teacher hungry to learn or a veteran teacher in search of a refresh, this pocket guide holds accessible solutions.

For the most part, many of us are familiar with the concept of colonization. We either learned the watered down and fictional version of our nation's colonial past, such as the false, joyful images of the first Thanksgiving, or we learned the blunt and accurate account of the genocide committed on Indigenous people who inhabited this land long before European arrival, in addition to the brutality and dehumanization of enslaved Africans. However, most teachers are less familiar with how our own classrooms, albeit to lesser degrees, have become colonized spaces.

This pocket guide posits that in many ways our classrooms enact oppression and it provides practical pathways for liberation. But it's not meant for all teachers! If you have not done the self work to understand the ways in which assorted aspects of your cultural identity impact your pedagogical decisions and the way you exist in the world, put this book down and do that first. If you haven't examined the privilege and power that your positionality presents in your daily interactions with young people and colleagues, put this book down and do that first. If you are not willing to continually interrogate and interrupt the ways in which you perpetuate dynamics of oppression, put this book down and do that first. I will be here when you get back! Two books that supported my initial self work are Terrell and Lindsay's *Culturally Proficient Leadership* and

Glenn Singleton's *Courageous Conversations about Race*. You may also refer to the recommended reading list found at the end of the book for more phenomenal texts to nurture your liberation of self and system's journey.

Now, assuming you have done your self work, let's begin! According to the New Oxford American Dictionary, colonization is defined as:

- the action or process of settling among and establishing control over the indigenous people of an area, and
- the action of appropriating a place or domain for one's own use (Oxford Dictionaries, 2022, s.v. "colonization").

Let's be honest, in most classrooms, teachers settle among, establish control over, and appropriate the classroom space for their own use. We may do it knowingly or unknowingly, intentionally or unintentionally, maliciously or meaning well, but we are doing it.

On the other hand, the New Oxford American Dictionary defines liberation as,

- the act of setting someone free from imprisonment, slavery, or oppression; release, and
- freedom from limits on thought or behavior (Oxford Dictionaries, 2022, s.v. "liberation").

Classrooms can be spaces of liberation for the young people we serve as well as for ourselves. My personal definition of a liberated space consists of AUTHENTICITY (people are able to be themselves), BELONGING (people are accepted, included, and cared for), and CREATIVITY (people are free to imagine, design, and manifest their hopes and dreams). In liberated education spaces, we can achieve freedom for self, others, systems and society. We have spent so much of our lives suffering from one form of oppression or another, so it is going to take time and intentionality to discover what it truly means to be personally free and professionally free. I say we, because liberation work is lifetime work and it is collective work. We must all actively liberate our thoughts and actions on a daily basis. And by doing our own liberation work, we will also create spaces that free young people from unnecessary limits on their thoughts and behavior in school.

Throughout the text, I intentionally use the terms "young person" and "young people" instead of "students" because it serves as a linguistic reinforcement of the whole humanity of the young people in our care. In the same way that "educator" is only one aspect of our complex identity, "student" is merely one aspect of a young person's identity. Young people hold many roles in their families, communities, and social circles, and their identities impact their lived experiences in society. What young people need most is for us to see them fully and respond to their wholeness with love and excellence.

As you read this pocket guide, I invite you to consider a few ways that you can design for liberation. Designing for liberation allows us to more fully realize our professional mission to do right by all young people, especially those from historically marginalized communities. Each chapter of this pocket guide will be organized in

"What? Why? How?" sections for clarity and ease of navigation. Each chapter will include resources for further exploration, and by no means are these exhaustive recommendations. When you see something <u>underlined</u>, it means that the URL for that recommended resource can be found in the Appendix. Each chapter will provide space for reflection and planning. Just remember, this pocket guide is an appetizer; you are the meal!

II. LIBERATE YOUR CONSCIOUSNESS!

II. Liberate Your Consciousness!
consciousness: the awareness or perception of something by a person

What?
A liberated consciousness is a consciousness that operates in (near) complete awareness of the sociopolitical context of self, the sociopolitical context of young people, and an understanding of the ways in which historical and current inequities impact culturally and linguistically diverse (CLD) young people.

Why?
Teachers and young people do not exist in a vacuum. We have been marinated in our alternately shared and siloed histories. These histories are important because they provide context and comprehension for the present. When we take time to gain a general knowledge of global, national, and local history and stay apprised of current events, we liberate our consciousness. We further liberate our conciousness by understanding intersectionality, or "the interconnected nature of social categorizations such as race, class, and gender as they apply to a given individual or group" and the way that our intersectional identities "create overlapping and interdependent systems of discrimination or disadvantage" (Oxford Dictionaries, 2022, s.v. "intersectionality"). Every aspect of our cultural identity, including but not limited to, age, gender, race, religion, sexual orientation, socioeconomic

status, physical/mental ability differences, and education level impacts the way we perceive the world, and the way we perform within it.

Our background shapes our beliefs and biases, which ultimately impact our behavior. **As teachers, we must acknowledge that our intersectional identities and background experiences shape the way we view and interact in the world, and therefore it's impossible for us to enter a space as "neutral."** Rather, we enter a space with bias and gaps of understanding that influence our teaching and our interactions with young people and colleagues.

The same is true for our young people. Young people enter their classroom spaces with their own biases, blind spots, and intersectional identities. To respond to their interests, passions, needs, and critique, we have to truly see and know them. We must choose to view them in their whole, integrated humanity. It's not that we all need to become history majors or experts in every single cultural identity marker. Rather, we must heed Paolo Friere's wise counsel to act as an artist of our young people's potential: "The teacher is of course an artist, but being an artist does not mean that he or she can make the profile, can shape the students. What the educator does in teaching is to make it possible for the students to become themselves" (Friere and Horton, 1990). As teachers we must integrate critical analysis, sense of agency, and critical action for young people's self actualization and societal progress.

How?
- ☐ Take time to reflect on your intersectional identities and the ways in which certain aspects of our identity manifest in societal advantages or disadvantages. Start by viewing this Privileged and Marginalized Identities handout. Highlight where you fall in both columns, and reflect on how your sociocultural identity markers and life experiences have shaped your beliefs about self, others, and the world. You can conduct a similar exercise with young people so that you can learn more about them, and they can learn more about each other. You can watch this Loom Video where I facilitated this process for a group of novice teachers. The password is *LIBERATE* (all caps).
- ☐ Kimberlé Crenshaw, who coined the term intersectionality, defines intersectional awareness as "understanding the ways that multiple forms of inequality or disadvantage sometimes compound themselves, and [how] they create obstacles that often are not understood within conventional ways of thinking about antiracism, or feminism, or whatever social structures we have" (NAIS, 2018). You can watch "The Urgency of Intersectionality" to get a deeper understanding of intersectional identities.
- ☐ Engage in Empathy Interviews to get to know your young people in four dimensions: as individuals, as learners, as family/community members, and as members of a complex

society. In each dimension, young people experience and witness varying degrees of oppression and opportunity. **If we begin to value the lived experience of the self as much as the learned experience from the shelf, we will not need young people or colleagues to compartmentalize aspects of their identity when they enter the school campus.** Rather, we can welcome their integrated identity and authentic selves in our learning spaces. Check out the "<u>Knowing Young People in Four Dimensions</u>" empathy interview that you can adapt and integrate into your practice.

- Diversify information and communication sources so that they include CLD voices. This includes integrating news, books, articles, podcasts, television series, social media, music, etc. For example <u>Black Effect podcast network</u>, <u>My Cultura podcast network</u>, <u>Media Indigena</u>, and <u>Asian Podcast network</u> are just a few podcast platforms that share diverse perspectives.
- Most importantly, we must establish and sustain relationships with human beings who have different lived experiences and perspectives than our own, in order to expand our sociopolitical awareness.

Resources
- Harvard Implicit Association Tests: The Implicit Association Test (IAT) measures attitudes and beliefs that people may be unwilling or unable to report. We can use these implicit association tests to examine our bias as it relates to race, gender, weight, etc.
- Critical consciousness: A key to student achievement: This article discusses the impact of critical consciousness in classrooms and provides three promising practices.
- Cultivating Critical Consciousness in the Classroom: Two researchers share insights and practices that surfaced as they observed teachers who integrate critical consciousness in their classrooms.
- Cultivating Critical Consciousness in the Classroom: 10 Counternarrative Resources: This article highlights the importance of counternarratives and the power of storytelling to nurture self-worth, empathy, and understanding.

DeLIBERATIONS!
long and careful considerations or discussions

What are you going to do to liberate your consciousness?

III. LIBERATE YOUR CLASSROOM!

III. Liberate Your Classroom!
classroom: a learning space

What?

A liberated classroom space is a flexible space that is conducive to cooperative learning and co-designed experiences. Cooperative learning is a cornerstone of many collectivist cultures. This is inherent in the Zulu philosophy of Ubuntu, "I am, because we are" and also in the Mayan moral code of In Lak'ech, "You are my other me." In a liberated classroom, we leverage the significance that collaboration and interdependence hold in many culturally and linguistically diverse (CLD) communities, and we include young people in the design of classroom experiences.

Why?

The vast majority of CLD young people are from collectivist cultures, which means many CLD young people have lived experiences working collaboratively. The interdependent nature of collectivist cultures means people work in groups and their purpose is to work for the overall benefit of the group. Community and societal benefits take precedence over individual desires, and productivity is often socially influenced. In individualist cultures, drive and productivity are often to improve or help the individual, while in collectivist cultures motivation and productivity is often for the good of the group. **In the same way that biodiversity strengthens a biological ecosystem,**

sociocultural diversity helps strengthen a classroom ecosystem. It allows young people to integrate multiple viewpoints and perspectives, resulting in a far more expansive knowledge base. It's that old philosophy, if I have one idea, and you have one idea, and we exchange ideas, now we both have two ideas! Collaboration serves as a multiplier of knowledge and experience which elevates young peoples' and teachers' collective impact.

How?
☐ Use flexible seating arrangements to experiment with various types of dialogue and interaction. Check out a few seating configurations from Dr. Todd Finley, co-author of <u>*Rethinking Classroom Design: Create Student-Centered Learning Spaces for 6-12th Graders*</u>

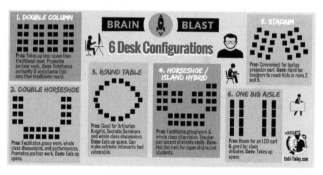

We can also explore learning spaces outside of the confines of four walls like museums, libraries, community organizations, and the most liberatory of all, the outdoors! Nature is a perpetual educator with limitless possibilities for learning. You might try a "Wonder Wander," where young people take a walk, observe the world, and write down any wonderings that surfaced that they would like to discuss and investigate. <u>Verdi Eco School</u> is a brilliant model of outdoor learning.

☐ We can incorporate multiple ways for our young people to engage in collaborative group work, design processes, and presentations. **One way to increase young people's agency in this process is to allow the group to co-construct community agreements to ensure that everyone's personal values are integrated.** This helps generate buy-in and shared accountability. For instance, in my classroom we co-constructed the 3 R's: respecting ourselves, respecting others, and respecting the environment, and our class co-constructed what that means and looks like for them, and how they want to *be with* one another. When doing project work, young people have been able to choose where to work, who to work with, and what to work on with the understanding that we can have fun and still be productive. (There are also times when I assigned groupings to help develop cross-cultural relationships among each other or to foster neurodiverse groupings.)

☐ Young people are not born knowing how to collaborate effectively in school. In traditional school settings, young people are socialized to avoid interdependence. So even if young people come from a collectivist household, the messages and the expectations at school are different. Additionally, young people from collectivist households may not know how to collaborate effectively with peers who have different values or customs. Young people who come from individualistic households also need help collaborating. It's important to invest time in the beginning of the school year supporting young people's ability to work together. We can engage young people in a series of community building exercises to launch cooperative learning through creative team challenges and culture building activities. This "Analyzing Groupwork videos and Co-Developing Group Norms" resource is a great exercise to explore the dynamics of group work. We can assign Group Roles that rotate so that young people gain familiarity with various elements of group participation. Be sure to conduct a debrief after each exercise so that they can reflect on their "Glows," what they are doing well, and "Grows," what they might improve, when it comes to group work.

☐ When we give young people frequent opportunities to work collaboratively, conflict is inevitable. As classroom liberators, we need to be able to acknowledge that different cultures and individuals respond to conflict differently. In some collectivist cultures negotiations are influenced by social harmony, while in many individualist cultures negotiations are influenced by personal well being outcomes. Part of being a liberatory educator is helping young people navigate the dynamics of group work through generative conflict. We maintain the culturally responsive integrity of our classroom by honoring the perspectives of all group members. One tip you might try is to have members of each group share openly (if they feel comfortable) about how conflict is resolved in their households. Young people can work together to co-create agreements about how they would like to resolve conflict in their learning group. I recommend having them do dialogical interviews using Elena Aguilar's <u>Reflecting on Conflict</u> prompts. And if you are a teacher of "littles" aka people younger than ten years old, you can use simple prompts such as, "What happens when someone disagrees with someone else in the family?" Or you might display a chart that shows different emotions, and have them share how their family responds when they feel this way.

☐ We can also expand our view of collaboration in the classroom space by thinking about ways to integrate families and communities into our curriculum design. For instance, at Back-to-School night, we can have a sign up sheet called, "Cool Things Caregivers Can Do" or "Caregiver Capacities," where parents, guardians, and caregivers can share their areas of expertise and contact information so that we can invite them to collaborate, teach, or offer expert critique.

Resources
- <u>National Equity Project's Liberatory Design Deck</u>: This deck offers mindsets and modes to design for equity.
- <u>Liberated Spaces: Purposeful School Design Says Goodbye to Cells and Bells</u>: This article discusses the power of fluid, flexible, and functional spaces that support liberatory learning.
- <u>Qualities of Regenerative and Liberatory Culture</u>: This article explores how nature can help us design cultures that are liberatory and healing.
- <u>Dismantling Oppression and Designing Liberation</u>: This graphic summarizes Kenneth Jones and Tema Okun's work on white supremacy culture and Daniel Lim's work on regenerative and liberatory qualities. It helps you identify and eliminate oppressive ways of being, as well as identify and emulate liberatory ways of being.
- <u>Educate to Liberate: Build an Anti-Racist Classroom</u>: This article discusses five classroom practices to liberate, transform and empower learning.
- <u>Characteristics of innovative learning spaces that you should know</u>: This article shares nine characteristics when designing learning centers and spaces.

DeLIBERATIONS!
long and careful considerations or discussions

What are you going to do to liberate your classroom?

IV. LIBERATE YOUR CURRICULUM!

IV. Liberate Your Curriculum!
curriculum: the subjects comprising a course of study in a school or college

What?

A liberated curriculum is a curriculum that represents, elevates, honors, and integrates all young peoples' cultural and linguistic backgrounds and cultural ways of being. A liberated curriculum is not Eurocentric in nature, nor is it isolated in social science courses. Rather, it provides multiple and diverse perspectives in all subject areas, including math and science. A liberated and culturally responsive approach to content means that we analyze what content our students are learning before we concern ourselves with content mastery. We have to discern whether the content we teach is perpetuating an ethnocentric view of the content area, or if it integrates diverse authors, experts, and contributors. Emily Style said, "education needs to enable the student to look through window frames in order to see the realities of others and into mirrors in order to see her/his own reality reflected" (Style, 1988). To put it plainly, a balanced and liberated curriculum includes mirrors and windows. It also infuses joy throughout the learning journey.

Why?

The University of Wisconsin-Madison School of Education Cooperative Children's Book Center's 2018 Diversity in Children's Books infographic is super telling. Animals still have more representation than all people of color combined!

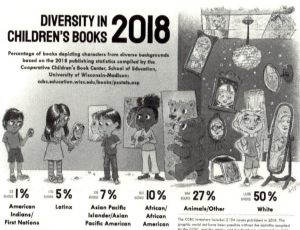

LGBTQ+, neurodiverse, or emergent bilingual protagonists. These omissions occur from kindergarten to college in literary works as well as textbooks. Poet Adrienne Rich said, "When someone with the authority of a teacher describes the world and you're not in it, there is a moment of psychic disequilibrium, as if you looked into a mirror and saw nothing." When we make discretionary decisions about who and what to include in our curriculum, the choice is not neutral. It is often steeped in bias. We are deciding what content is worthy of mastery. We are deciding who and what is included or excluded. These decisions have the power to reveal narrow or expanded worldviews, to impede or empower, to damage or heal. There is deep psychological damage inflicted on young people who do not see themselves in the curriculum. While it may be tempting to believe this only applies to English Language Arts or Social Science courses, that is not the case. Diverse representation is essential and imperative in all subject areas-math and science especially given their disproportionate inclusion and representation of Black, Indigenous, Latinx, and women. And it can be achieved via direct instruction and collaborative learning.

When culturally and linguistically diverse (CLD) young people are continually confronted with content that does not include exemplars, historical figures, scientists, mathematicians, or models of excellence who look like them, or when representations of their cultural identity are overwhelmingly negative, it has harmful impacts on their self and cultural group perception (Pledger, 2018). At the same time, all young people enhance their understanding of others when content provides them with windows into the experiences of others. Exposure is an essential step toward the development of empathy, or the ability to understand and share the feelings of another. **Content that elevates the cross-cultural triumphs and inequities faced by individuals genuinely merits mastery, as it impacts positive racial identity development and community compassion.** How we create and deliver curriculum truly matters. Our curriculum can either transfer content from one repository to another or it can transform young people's reflections about themselves, others, and the world around them.

How?
- ☐ We can commit to a process of learning, unlearning, and relearning when it comes to writing or choosing curriculum. Center our young peoples' sociocultural identities first and foremost in our courses. For instance, social science teachers will need to reject the common practice of Eurocentric history as a required course, and Black and Latinx history as electives. English Language Arts teachers will need to assign books by diverse authors and with diverse protagonists. Math and science teachers will need to research and elevate CLD mathematicians and scientists who have made significant contributions in their fields. Teachers of art, language, or computer science will need to elevate the work and expertise of women, people of color, LGBTQ+ community, neurodivergent community and more.
- ☐ Design learning experiences that are relevant and applicable to CLD young peoples' lived experiences. This not only develops a positive sense of identity, it increases the likelihood of content integration and mastery. In most cases, to achieve mastery in a content area, a young person needs to care enough about

the subject matter to invest time, energy, and effort to develop expertise. In contextualized learning, content mastery is evidenced by skillful application of the concept or skill. Whether it's social science lessons that center on a current election, math lessons about the exponential growth in the use of vape pens, or science lessons that examine the water quality in their neighborhoods, relevant inquiry-based learning can be meaningful and memorable. I encourage you to check out High Tech High Graduate School of Education's <u>Unboxed Cards</u> and EL Educations <u>Models of Excellence</u> for more ideas on how to do this in your content area.

☐ Include young people in a co-construction of curriculum by inviting their input through surveys, focus groups, or whole class ideation sessions. Chris Emdin's "<u>7C's for effective teaching</u>" aka Reality Pedagogy model is a great place to start. Provide opportunities for young people to share from their funds of knowledge, or their personal knowledge, skills, and life experience, which will expand content coverage while reducing status differentials. Young people learn by doing, by experiencing, and by applying their learning in current and future contexts. It is up to us to design or co-design these meaningful moments of mastery for and with the beautifully diverse humans in our care.

Resources
- How Schools and Teachers Can Get Better at Cultural Competence: This article introduces practices that teachers and school leaders can employ to improve cultural competence.
- Teaching Toward Genius: An Equity Model For Pedagogy In Action: This article discusses Dr. Gholdy Muhammad's Histories, Identities, Literacies and Liberation (HILL) model as an equity framework for teaching and learning across all differences. The HILL model helps teachers design for five key learning pursuits: identity, skill, intellectualism, criticality, and joy.
- Curriculum as Window and Mirror: This paper discusses the need for curriculum to function as both a window and a mirror in order to reflect and reveal the multicultural world in which we live.
- Curriculum as Encounter: This article discusses the importance of integrating the life-text of young people and recognizing how their lived experiences shape their perceptions of the world.
- Backwards Design Template: This template supports the design and co-design of student-centered projects and units that lead to enduring understanding.
- The following are websites with lesson plans, simulations, classroom activities, resources and more!
  - Zinn Education Project Teaching Materials
  - Woke Kindergarten
  - Science in the City

- Social Justice Math
- Abolitionist Teaching Network Resources for Agitators
- Teaching Tolerance Classroom Resources
- Facing History and Ourselves Educator Resources

DeLIBERATIONS!
long and careful considerations or discussions

What are you going to do to liberate your curriculum?

V. LIBERATE YOUR COGNITIVE CAPACITY BIAS!

GENDER, RACE, AND SOCIOECONOMIC STATUS DO NOT DETERMINE YOUR MATH ABILITY.

WE'RE ALL MATHEMATICIANS IN THIS CLASS!

V. Liberate Your Cognitive Capacity Bias!
cognitive capacity: having well-developed cognitive skills essential to learning

bias: prejudice in favor of or against one thing, person, or group compared with another, usually in a way considered to be unfair

What?

A liberated cognitive capacity bias means we believe in the cognitive ability or potential of all our young people. It means we are confident in each and every young person's ability to engage in critical thinking and complex problem solving regardless of their sociocultural background. It also means we are committed to shifting culturally and linguistically diverse (CLD) young people from dependent learners to independent learners.

Why?

When it comes to teaching CLD young people, many educators, consciously or unconsciously, hold deficit beliefs about their abilities, potential, and achievement capability. Those beliefs are influenced by our own background experiences, the media, and societal constructs. Historically, deficit mindsets have contributed to policies and practices like IQ tests, tracking, sheltered classrooms, and the labeling and categorization of young people in harmful ways that ultimately impact educational opportunities and life outcomes. **When we possess deficit thinking**

about CLD young peoples' academic abilities, it often leads to over scaffolding and lowering of rigor on the part of the teacher, and learned helplessness on the part of the young person.

In his article "When Love is Grounded in the Soft Bigotry of Low Expectations, It's the Wrong Kind of Love," Colin Seale describes the danger and damage of deficit thinking. When we deny young people the "glory of productive struggle," it is the "easy" way out for both them and their teachers. Lowering our expectations does a tremendous disservice to young people's long term cognitive and behavioral development. It also prevents teachers from developing their cognitive coaching skills. When CLD young people remain in a dependent state, they constantly depend on their teacher's instruction or their peers' guidance to move forward. This makes it difficult for them to problem-solve independently. Being unable to take initiative and direct their own learning negatively impacts their future academic and career aspirations, not to mention their own feelings of intellectual capacity and self-determining agency.

Teacher and researcher Zaretta Hammond discusses several deficit thinking mindsets in her book, *Culturally Responsive Teaching and the Brain*. One of these mindsets, which she calls "Pobrecito Syndrome," happens when teachers feel so sorry for young people, their home life, and their perceived ability level, that we lower rigor in order to build young people's self-esteem. Another deficit thinking mindset is "Myth of

Meritocracy," when teachers hold the belief that all young people have the same access and their success is entirely based on their own effort and grit. According to this mindset, young people just need to work harder to succeed; if they fail, it's on them. In both of these scenarios, young people are not learning because their teacher has robbed them of productive struggle, and taken away their opportunity to build cognitive capacity in a supportive environment.

Similar to productive struggle, renowned educator and author James Nottingham talks about the cognitive conflict that occurs in what he refers to as "The Learning Pit," a critical space during learning when a learner feels challenged, confused, or stuck (Nottingham, 2015). Over scaffolding, reducing rigor, or failing young people in the "learning pit" is an avoidable disservice to them. Recognizing and regulating our own deficit beliefs frees us from those debilitating mindsets and makes us mindful of what young people are capable of achieving. We are now liberated to create conditions for critical thinking and problem solving in our classroom that develops the intellective capacity of CLD young people. Competence, not compliments, builds confidence. The more successful ascents out of the learning pit young people have, the more cognitive muscles they will build.

How?
☐ Once we humbly admit that we possess one or more of these mindsets, we can take steps

to replace the deficit-thinking with asset-based perspectives of all of our young people. Sometimes this might mean redefining what we honor as an asset. **We may need to reject dominant culture views regarding what is considered significant, what is valued as intelligent, or what process path is deemed appropriate by honoring the funds of knowledge young people carry with them on a daily basis.** Diverse youth possess multiple forms of cultural capital like navigational capital, linguistic capital, or aspirational capital, as described in Tara Yosso's, "<u>Whose culture has capital? A critical race theory discussion of community cultural wealth</u>." Cultural capital leads to divergent ways of thinking about and solving complex problems, as well as different ways of approaching a pressing problem or innovative opportunity.

☐ Let's turn to Zaretta Hammond again for some sage advice, "As culturally responsive teachers, we have a particular duty to help dependent learners build their intellective capacity so that they are able to do more independent learning and higher order thinking...the first step toward independent learning is acquiring the tools to be more data driven in ones decision-making about learning tactics and strategies" (Hammond, 2015). For this to take place we need to connect with young people, establish and maintain relational trust, then mutually enter into a learning partnership that aligns both teachers and young people as co-conspirators of cognitive ability development. Some of us might envision it as a gradual release method, whereby instructional coaching and implementation of cognitive routines can help move young people toward greater independence. We can help young people be increasingly independent learners by providing scaffolds for how to organize data, checklists to track progress, time and brave space to process content and posit questions, opportunities to engage in critique and revision cycles, criteria for how to engage in credible research, and co-constructed problem solving tips.

☐ Design learning experiences that provide opportunities for young people to engage in "productive struggle", or what James Nottingham calls "cognitive conflict," occasions when they can grapple with complex questions, investigate concepts, and wrestle with contradictions in a way that develops their cognitive muscles.

Resources
- Author Interview With Dr. Gholdy Muhammad: 'Cultivating Genius': In this interview, Dr. Gholdy Muhammad discusses her historically and culturally responsive equity framework and more.
- A Conversation about Instructional Equity with Zaretta Hammond: In this interview, Zaretta Hammond shares her perspective on the distinction between multicultural education, social justice education, and culturally responsive pedagogy.
- The Neuroscience Behind Productive Struggle: This article introduces four strategies to introduce productive struggle in the classroom
- The Learning Pit: In this video, James Nottingham provides a very clear example of how to engage young people in productive struggle.
- When Students Seem Stalled: This article is about helping students connect new information to prior knowledge and become self-directed learners through the use of cognitive structures.

DeLIBERATIONS!
long and careful considerations or discussions

What are you going to do to liberate your cognitive capacity bias?

VI. LIBERATE YOUR COMMUNICATION

VI. Liberate Your Communication!
communication: the imparting or exchanging of information or news; the successful conveying or sharing of ideas and feelings; means of connection between people or places, in particular

What?

A liberated approach to communication means we are aware of the fact that verbal and non-verbal communication styles vary across cultures. As liberated communicators, we appreciate the benefits and sophistication of multilingualism and code-switching, and we advocate inclusive language. These commitments are evident in our modes of communication as well as in our quality of communication.

Why?

Transactional communication is meant to impart or exchange information and this can be done in a variety of ways: speaking, writing, listening, images, music, body language, etc. The United Nations recognizes more than 6,000 spoken languages, not to mention the various dialects within those languages. When we consider all forms of non-verbal communication, it is quite clear that there are a plethora of ways to communicate, yet this term is often thought of in the very narrow terms of speaking, writing, and listening, and often based on Eurocentric measures. This widely accepted, limited view of communication leads culturally and linguistically diverse young people to engage in linguistic and/

or situational code-switching to varying degrees of success. **Teachers send mixed messages when we praise white young people for learning a new language and reprimand Latinx young people for speaking Spanish in the classroom. Bilingualism is a superpower. It's an asset and should be treated as such.** Similarly, a young person's ability to code-switch is a survival tactic because it affords them the ability to maintain social standing in different cultural settings. A question to consider is: why should young people have to employ their code-switching superpower in the first place?

Transformative communication seeks to create positive change in human development. Examining communication competence through a liberated and cultural lens means that educators appreciate, or at the very least, acknowledge diverse cultural forms of communication. It is important to attend to which forms of communication are given status in the classroom. When we frame Standard American English as a superior form of communication, we are reinforcing assimilation. *How to be an Antiracist* author Ibram X Kendi likens assimilation to telling someone they are "temporarily inferior," a message that is damaging to the positive cultural identity development of young people. When we liberate communication, we include and honor diverse modes of input and output to prompt young people to think, reflect, and share their learning, while acknowledging how various forms of communication determine access and opportunity in society.

If we want to further create an environment of trust and belonging in our classroom, the quality of our communication also matters. The words and phrases we use or allow to be used in our classroom environment contribute to young peoples' sense of safety and sense of belonging. This is yet another set of discretionary decisions that have the ability to promote or prohibit equity. Take a moment to reflect on the power of words in your own life. What words have you heard that were uplifting? What words have you heard that were damaging? In our profession there is a young human being on the other side of our words, and our words have lasting impact which is why liberated communication truly matters.

How?
- ☐ Pronounce young peoples' names correctly. If we want all of our young people to have a sense of belonging, taking the time to learn how to say their names correctly honors a core part of their identity.
- ☐ Acknowledge and celebrate the power of emergent bilinguals and effective code-switchers, and interrogate the ways in which language operates as a tool of power and privilege in our society.
- ☐ Integrate inclusive communication into our daily vocabulary and phrasing. When we think about the complex intersectionality of our young people, we realize that we

have numerous opportunities to create an exclusive or inclusive learning environment. Asking young people their pronouns, using ability-based language, and language that includes experiences of diverse socio-economic statuses are just a few ways to ensure inclusive communication. The Bank Street School for Children created <u>Language Values</u> that are useful for educators hoping to model communication that fosters a sense of belonging.

☐ **Don't make assumptions about young peoples' ability or intelligence level if and when their communication style is different from our own.** Communication styles differ based on culture, and also vary from family to family. Some young people respond better to clear directives that mirror styles in their own homes, while others benefit from interrogative coaxing. The best way for a teacher to decipher what communication style is more effective is to get to know the young people within their care.

Resources
- Getting it right; why pronouncing names correctly matters: In this Ted Talk, Gerardo Ochoa shares a personal story about the impact of pronouncing names incorrectly.
- Facundo the Great: In this short video Ramon "Chunky" Sanchez shares an endearing story about the importance of pronouncing names correctly.
- Bank Street School for Children Language Values: These are sample language shifts that create a more inclusive culture.
- Say Less: a Lesson in Code Switching: In this Ted Talk, Naya Stevens discusses the complexities and merits of code switching.
- To Code Switch or Not to Code Switch: In this Ted Talk high school student, Katelynn Duggins shares how she navigates code switching.
- The Silenced Dialogue: Power and Pedagogy in Education Other People's Children: This article discusses the codes of power that young people are expected to navigate in education.

DeLIBERATIONS!
long and careful considerations or discussions

What are you going to do to liberate your communication?

VII. LIBERATE YOUR CONDUCT CONSTRUCTS!

VII. Liberate Your Conduct Constructs!
conduct: the manner in which a person behaves, especially on a particular occasion or in a particular context

construct: an idea or theory containing various conceptual elements, typically one considered to be subjective and not based on empirical evidence

What?
A liberated approach to conduct constructs or approaches to disciplinary infractions separates the deed from the doer. It places emphasis on building authentic relationships, seeking to understand young peoples' motives for behavior, and understanding the role of brain development when we are faced with unexpected behaviors. It also means that we co-construct conduct expectations. We ground natural and logical consequences in young people's social success and engagement in community culture, rather than relying on predetermined school policy or adult power to force young people to conform to our expectations.

Why?
Traditional responses to disciplinary infractions like zero-tolerance policies contribute to opportunity gaps because they interrupt a young person's attendance, academic access and social interactions, which negatively impacts academic achievement. When a young person is absent from our classroom, she misses

out on content, classroom connection, and becomes increasingly disengaged. Once she feels disconnected from the learning environment, she may wrongfully or prematurely assume that school is "not for her". Unfortunately, it's all connected, as learning gaps impact opportunity gaps which impact achievement gaps. Declines in academic achievement, engagement, and sense of belonging increase the likelihood of a young person dropping out of high school (Pledger, 2018). Suspension from school not only disrupts academic learning and a positive school culture, it can increase the likelihood of a young person being asked to repeat the grade, which in turn increases the likelihood of dropping out of school.

This increased probability of dropping out of school or interfacing with the juvenile justice system places young people on a criminal path to prison instead of a college path to a profession. Oppressive discipline policies play an integral role in diminished opportunities for historically marginalized young people, and it starts at a very early age. Dr. Luke Wood stated that, "the highest rates of suspension disparity, it's not in high school, it's not in middle school, it's not even in latter elementary. It's in early childhood education, kindergarten through third grade where black boys are 522% more likely to be suspended than their peers" (Hong, 2021). This is a problem.

How did these inequities come to fruition in our classrooms? Implicit bias, stereotypes, racial tension, and teachers' and administrators' cultural insensitivity are the main culprits of these inequities on school campuses.* **When implicit bias and cultural incompetence are present, it is quite possible for teachers to knowingly and unknowingly engage in discriminatory discipline practices that negatively impact young people.** The discretionary aspect of discipline policies creates subjective situations in which we discipline students based on our own biases. This makes it possible for inexperience, prejudice, and even retaliation to become a factor in the disciplinary decisions of teachers and administrators, which negatively impacts young people, especially those from marginalized backgrounds.

How?
- ☐ Keep young people in class with us! The easy route is to outsource "the problem" by sending young people to the office, the dean, the counselor, or some other adult in the hope that they solve "the problem." When navigating a behavioral challenge with a young person, before jumping to conclusions, let's ask ourselves, "what else might be true?" We can check the stories we are telling ourselves about the young person. We can actively seek out different stories that may explain why they are doing what they are doing. We can try to discern what needs they are trying to express. We have an opportunity to rewrite the story, repair relationships, and

move toward learning and healing.
- ☐ Utilize compassionate curiosity to get at the root cause of disruptive and/or destructive behavior by knowing our young people. Every behavior expresses a need, thus it falls to the adults in the learning environment to discern, then respond to the needs of our young people. This takes time, especially when a young person may have had a history of educator neglect or dismissal and exhibit low levels of trust, belonging, and psychological safety. Exclusion from the community should only be employed when the young person is causing severe harm to themselves or others, and when all other avenues of restoration have been intentionally and systematically explored.
- ☐ Evaluate and redesign teaching and learning that engages young people and develops their academic mindsets by taking the time to cultivate learning partnerships. One strategy that can help address class attendance, improve successful course completion, and reduce the number of disciplinary infractions, is for educators to reexamine and reimagine the classroom experience. Engaging pedagogy has the ability to reduce chronic absenteeism, increase content knowledge, and improve skill development. When young people enjoy learning, they want to be present, and when they are present they are exposed to more content and have time to develop an array of skills. In addition

to academic benefits, engaging pedagogy can help reduce the number of referrals, suspensions, and expulsions because young people begin to feel more connected to the community. Whether it is project-based learning, problem-based learning, service learning, or another education innovation, when educators make a concerted effort to make classroom experiences relevant and rigorous, young people are less likely to get into trouble. When educators lean into cultivating strong <u>Academic Mindsets</u> such as "I belong in the academic community, I can succeed at this work, this work has value and purpose for me, and my abilities can grow with effort", young people can develop a completely different perspective on their personal education.

- ☐ Cultivate culturally responsive teaching self-efficacy. When young people begin to experience this combination of cultural competence and confidence, they develop additional positive habits that contribute to marked improvements in behavioral choices. For instance, studies indicate that incorporating culturally responsive pedagogy resulted in increased attendance and decreased disciplinary infractions (Pledger, 2018). The research demonstrates that when young peoples' cultural heritage is acknowledged and honored, they are more inclined to feel a sense of belonging that motivates them to refrain from negative behavior patterns (Pledger,

2018). Young people who were previously characterized by their negative reputation were able to reverse the narrative and change their academic trajectory once they began to view themselves and their cultural identity in a positive light.

☐ Implement proper and ongoing Restorative Justice (RJ) training or Positive Behavior Interventions and Supports (PBIS) to replace zero-tolerance policies. Without proper training, PBIS is often misapplied as a system of extrinsic rewards while Restorative Justice frequently becomes an exercise of performative absolution. However, when properly implemented, both approaches teach young people about the impact of their actions on the community. Simply providing faculty with an isolated professional development training that does not give teachers the opportunity to experience or simulate the practices can lead to regression to the mean instead of restoration of the relationships. Continuous coaching that involves investigating the root causes of behavior, role-play, dialogue, and an opportunity to address real-time classroom concerns will yield far more positive results than a book or workshop.

Resources
- National Center for Restorative Justice: The National Center for Restorative Justice is focused on training those interested in changing their relationship with conflict, in particular those who serve youth.
- Center on Positive Behavioral Interventions and Supports: The Center on Positive Behavioral Interventions and Supports provides an evidence-based three tiered framework to improve and integrate data, systems, and practices to improve student outcomes.
Restorative Justice: Resources for Schools:
- Explore resources and case studies that demonstrate how to bring restorative justice to your school or classroom.
- Leading Equity Center Podcast: How to connect restorative practices and social and emotional learning: This podcast episode discusses the relationship between restorative justice and social-emotional learning and how to integrate them in schools.
- Restorative Practices for Guide for Educators: This toolkit introduces educators to restorative practices and how the practices contribute to a safe and positive learning environment.

A perspective from my copy-editor, Krista Galleberg, that is beyond the scope of this book but one that I believe is worthy of consideration: The inequities of school mirror the inequities of society. Unfortunately, most schools are amplifying those inequities rather than mitigating them. For example, Black children are statistically more likely to live in poverty because of residential segregation and economic racism. American poverty breeds violence because of our policies on guns and social services - so it might be true that Black children, on average, come to school more likely to get in fights. We are products of our circumstances. What are schools going to do about THAT problem? That's a different problem than bias.

Like Dr. Bettina Love says - teachers have to be more than allies, we must be CO-CONSPIRATORS for justice (Love, 2019). We need to do more than simply interrupt our own biases within the classroom. We need to also help create a world in which students are not facing extreme poverty and violence outside of school by building relationships with other colleagues, families, and community leaders. As we work to liberate our own classroom spaces, we must also remember that we are caught up in a larger system of social and historical inequity, if only to counteract any notions of saviorism or silver bullet solutions that we may have. We can interrupt our own biases, and that's a vital first step, and it won't solve all of the underlying societal inequities that we and our young people experience.

DeLIBERATIONS!
long and careful considerations or discussions

What are you going to do to liberate your conduct constructs?

VIII. ~~CONCLUSION~~ CALL TO COMMUNITY ACTION

VIII. ~~Conclusion~~ Call to Community Action
call to action: an exhortation or stimulus to do something in order to achieve an aim or deal with a problem

Phew! You made it! You now have a deeper understanding of how to liberate your consciousness, classroom, curriculum, cognitive capacity bias, communication and conduct constructs, as well as resources to put liberatory practices into action in each of these domains. I invite you to do this work in community with others by forming liberation groups, practicing these pocket-sized paradigms, and holding each other lovingly accountable to the just nurturing of young people. In this way, liberation can spill out of classrooms into schools, out of schools into communities, and out of communities into wider society!

This may be the conclusion of this pocket guide, but my hope is that this is a renewal of your commitment to liberatory learning so that all young people feel seen, heard, valued, supported and challenged in their classroom spaces. The reflections, recommendations, and resources I shared are merely a snapshot of what's possible as you move to liberatory learning. I encourage you to luxuriate in a learner mindset by asking questions, challenging your assumptions, and most importantly, listening to your young people, even when they do not have the exact words to express what they need. Your ability to notice, name, and navigate trusting and healthy learning partnerships with young people can have a dramatic impact on their present and future quality of life.

Our young people deserve to be embraced with love and freedom on a daily basis, and so do we! When we faithfully believe in the unquestionable worth and unlimited potential of young people, and our behaviors demonstrate that belief, we are on a path toward true liberation!

Appendix

"7C's for effective teaching" aka Reality Pedagogy model (https://www.ascd.org/el/articles/seven-cs-for-effective-teaching)

A Conversation about Instructional Equity with Zaretta Hammond (https://www.collaborativeclassroom.org/blog/a-conversation-about-instructional-equity-with-zaretta-hammond/)

Abolitionist Teaching Network Resources for Agitators (https://abolitionistteachingnetwork.org/resources-for-agitators)

Academic Mindsets (https://www.scoe.org/blog_files/Academic%20Mindsets.pdf)

"Analyzing Groupwork videos and Co-Developing Group Norms" (https://docs.google.com/document/d/14iEYFO9tL3OrDqRXcYzjXD9goPd0MiRNFIHTofzVjXU/edit?usp=sharing)

Asian Podcast Network https://www.justlikemedia.com/show/asian-podcast-network-the-podcast/

Author Interview With Dr. Gholdy Muhammad: 'Cultivating Genius' (https://www.edweek.org/teaching-learning/opinion-author-interview-with-dr-gholdy-muhammad-cultivating-genius/2020/01)

Backwards Design Template (https://docs.google.com/document/d/1lTGC_QCLlII2I-c9h9c8L8jCmvCyPJMo2WYI1xWqxnQ/edit?usp=sharing)

Bank Street School for Children Language Values (https://educate.bankstreet.edu/cgi/viewcontent.cgi?article=1036&context=faculty-staff)

Black Effect Podcast Network https://www.blackeffect.com/

Center on Positive Behavioral Interventions and Supports (https://www.pbis.org/)

Characteristics of innovative learning spaces that you should know (https://www.nuiteq.com/company/blog/characteristics-of-innovative-learning-spaces-that-you-should-know)

Critical consciousness: A key to student achievement (https://kappanonline.org/critical-consciousness-key-student-achievement/)

Cultivating Critical Consciousness in the Classroom (https://facingtoday.facinghistory.org/cultivating-critical-consciousness-in-the-classroom)

Cultivating Critical Consciousness in the Classroom: 10 Counternarrative Resources (https://www.gettingsmart.com/2021/02/15/cultivating-critical-consciousness-in-the-classroom-ten-counternarrative-resources/)

Cultivating Genius (https://shop.scholastic.com/teachers-ecommerce/teacher/books/cultivating-genius-an-equity-framework-9781338594898.html)

Culturally Responsive Teaching and the Brain (https://us.corwin.com/en-us/nam/culturally-responsive-teaching-and-the-brain/book241754)

Curriculum as Encounter (https://nationalseedproject.org/images/documents/Curriculum_as_Encounter.pdf)

Curriculum as Window and Mirror (https://nationalseedproject.org/images/documents/Curriculum_As_Window_and_Mirror.pdf)

Dismantling Oppression/Designing Liberation (https://drive.google.com/file/d/1ztunTjMjh4-1fD7impwuYGYIawsYA1uo/view?usp=sharing)

Educate to Liberate: Build an Anti-Racist Classroom (https://www.edutopia.org/blog/build-an-anti-racist-classroom-joshua-block)

EL Educations Models of Excellence (https://modelsofexcellence.eleducation.org/projects)

Facing History and Ourselves Educator Resources (https://www.facinghistory.org/educator-resources)

Facundo the Great (https://www.youtube.com/watch?v=s8FheuSE7w4)

Getting it right; why pronouncing names correctly matters (https://www.ted.com/talks/gerardo_ochoa_getting_it_right_why_pronouncing_names_correctly_matters)

Group roles template (https://docs.google.com/document/d/1-SA4eIG4oeQ_XPcy51ORVWEkHSb-5FzayLQZBmIuAdU/edit?usp=sharing)

Harvard Implicit Association Tests (https://implicit.harvard.edu/implicit/takeatest.html)

How Schools and Teachers Can Get Better at Cultural Competence (https://www.educationnext.org/how-schools-teachers-can-get-better-cultural-competence/)

Picture This: Diversity in Children's Books 2018 Infographic (https://readingspark.wordpress.com/2019/06/19/picture-this-diversity-in-childrens-books-2018-infographic/)

Knowing Young People in Four Dimensions (https://docs.google.com/document/d/1WHungw3icYqKsW6J2_cHyTfbZaI6yHvOrmy3W0KQyiQ/edit?usp=sharing)

Language Values (https://educate.bankstreet.edu/cgi/viewcontent.cgi?article=1036&context=faculty-staff)

Leading Equity Center Podcast: How to connect restorative practices and social and emotional learning (https://www.leadingequitycenter.com/130)

Liberated Spaces: Purposeful School Design Says Goodbye to Cells and Bells (https://www.edcan.ca/articles/liberated-spaces-purposeful-school-design-says-goodbye-to-cells-and-bells/)

National Center for Restorative Justice (http://www.nationalcenterforrestorativejustice.com/)

National Equity Project's Liberatory Design Deck (https://drive.google.com/file/d/1Kum0KDUqkysGrdkc2SfHXH4INY6RPEVG/view?usp=sharing)

Media Indigena (https://mediaindigena.com/)

My Cultura Podcast network (https://www.iheart.com/podcast/1299-my-cultura-podcasts-86658576/)

Privileged and Marginalized Identities (https://drive.google.com/file/d/10S5p4xgp1p45Jt_ulNOSWJSmF4jJ0DPH/view?usp=sharing)

Privileged and Marginalized Identities Sample lesson Loom Video (https://www.loom.com/share/919b1d8af0ce479e9d7071392979c31e) (Password LIBERATE)

Qualities of Regenerative and Liberatory Culture (https://regenerative.medium.com/qualities-of-regenerative-and-liberating-culture-9d3809b30557)

Reflecting on Conflict (https://brightmorning.wpengine.com/wp-content/uploads/2018/10/Exhibit-12.1-Reflecting-on-Conflict.pdf)

Restorative Justice: Resources for Schools (https://www.edutopia.org/blog/restorative-justice-resources-matt-davis#:~:text=Restorative%20justice%20empowers%20students%20to,questions%2C%20and%20air%20their%20grievances)

Rethinking Classroom Design: Create Student-Centered Learning Spaces for 6-12th Graders (https://rowman.com/ISBN/9781475818536/Rethinking-Classroom-Design-Create-Student-Centered-Learning-Spaces-for-6-12th-Graders)

Say Less: a Lesson in Code Switching (https://www.ted.com/talks/naya_stevens_say_less_a_lesson_in_code_switching)
Science in the City (https://scienceinthecity.stanford.edu/resources/)

Social Justice Math (https://justequations.org/resource/social-justice-math-in-action-webinar/)

Teaching Tolerance Classroom Resources (https://www.tolerance.org/classroom-resources)

Teaching Toward Genius: An Equity Model For Pedagogy In Action (https://ace-ed.org/teaching-toward-genius-an-equity-model-for-pedagogy-in-action/)

The Learning Pit (https://www.youtube.com/watch?v=3IMUAOhuO78)

The Neuroscience Behind Productive Struggle (https://www.edutopia.org/article/neuroscience-behind-productive-struggle)

The Silenced Dialogue: Power and Pedagogy in Education Other People's Children (http://lmcreadinglist.pbworks.com/f/Delpit+(1988).pdf)

"The Urgency of Intersectionality" (https://www.youtube.com/watch?v=akOe5-UsQ2o)
To Code Switch or Not to Code Switch (https://www.youtube.com/watch?v=sncGGjaYJ5I)

Unboxed Cards (https://hthunboxed.org/project-card-home/)

Unboxed Cards (https://hthunboxed.org/project-card-home/)

Verdi Eco School (https://www.verdiecoschool.org/)

When Love is Grounded in the Soft Bigotry of Low Expectations, It's the Wrong Kind of Love (https://educationpost.org/when-love-is-grounded-in-the-soft-bigotry-of-low-expectations-its-the-wrong-kind-of-love/)

"When Students Seem Stalled" (https://www.ascd.org/el/articles/when-students-seem-stalled)

Whose culture has capital? A critical race theory discussion of community cultural wealth" (https://thrive.arizona.edu/sites/default/files/Whose%20culture%20has%20capital_A%20critical%20race%20theory%20discussion%20of%20community%20cultural%20wealth_1.pdf)

Woke Kindergarten (https://www.zinnedproject.org/materials)

Zinn Education Project Teaching Materials (https://www.zinnedproject.org/materials)

References

A conversation about instructional equity with Zaretta Hammond. Center for the Collaborative Classroom. (2021, November 22). Retrieved December 23, 2021, from https://www.collaborativeclassroom.org/blog/a-conversation-about-instructional-equity-with-zaretta-hammond/

Abolitionist Teaching Network. (n.d.). Resources for agitators. Abolitionist Teaching Network. Retrieved December 23, 2021, from https://abolitionistteachingnetwork.org/resources-for-agitators

Adapted from the Social Justice Training. (n.d.). Privileged and Marginalized Identities. Retrieved December 23, 2021, from https://drive.google.com/file/d/10S5p4xgp1p45Jt_u1NOSWJSmF4jJ0DPH/view

Aguilar, E. (2016). "Reflecting on Conflict" from The Art of Coaching Teams: Building Resilient Communities that Transform Schools. Jossey-Bass.

Anaissie, T., Cary, V., Malarkey, T., & Wise, S. (n.d.). Liberatory Design Deck. National Equity Project . Retrieved December 23, 2021, from https://drive.google.com/file/d/1Kum0KDUqkysGrdkc2SfHXH4INY6RPEVG/view

Asian Podcast Network: The podcast. (n.d.). Retrieved December 30, 2021, from https://www.justlikemedia.com/show/asian-podcast-network-the-podcast/

Balaguru , S., & Canady, A. (2021). LE 130: How to connect restorative practices and social and emotional learning with dr. Soundhari Balaguru and Asha Canady. Home Page. Retrieved December 23, 2021, from https://www.leadingequitycenter.com/130

Bank Street School for Children. (2018, October). Language values at Bank Street - educate.bankstreet.edu. Retrieved December 23, 2021, from https://educate.bankstreet.edu/cgi/viewcontent.cgi?article=1036&context=faculty-staff&_ga=2.30674617.78890662.1581375350-103923623.1581375350

Billions Institute and Equity Meets Design. (2021). Dismantling Oppression and Designing Liberation. Retrieved December 23, 2021, from https://drive.google.com/file/d/1ztunTjMjh4-1fD7impwuYGYIawsYA1uo/view

Black effect. Black Effect. (n.d.). Retrieved December 30, 2021, from https://www.blackeffect.com/

Block, J. (2015, January 12). Educate to liberate: Build an anti-racist classroom. Edutopia. Retrieved December 23, 2021, from https://www.edutopia.org/blog/build-an-anti-racist-classroom-joshua-block

Center on PBIS. (n.d.). Retrieved December 23, 2021, from https://www.pbis.org/

Classroom resources. Learning for Justice. (2021). Retrieved December 26, 2021, from https://www.learningforjustice.org/classroom-resources

Dahlen, S. P. (2020, September 1). Picture this: Diversity in children's Books 2018 infographic. 박사라 Sarah Park Dahlen, Ph.D. Retrieved December 23, 2021, from https://readingspark.wordpress.com/2019/06/19/picture-this-diversity-in-childrens-books-2018-infographic/

Davis, M. (2015, October 29). Restorative justice: Resources for schools. Edutopia. Retrieved December 26, 2021, from https://www.edutopia.org/blog/restorative-justice-resources-matt-davis#:~:text=Restorative%20justice%20empowers%20students%20to,questions%2C%20and%20air%20their%20grievances

Delpit, L. (1988). The Silenced Dialogue: Power and Pedagogy in Educating Other People's Children. Harvard Educational Review; Aug 1988; 58, 3; Research Library pg. 280

Educator resources. Facing History and Ourselves. (n.d.). Retrieved December 23, 2021, from https://www.facinghistory.org/educator-resources

EL Education. (n.d.). Models of excellence. | Models of Excellence. Retrieved December 23, 2021, from https://modelsofexcellence.eleducation.org/projects

El-Amin, A., Seider, S., Graves, D., Tamerat, J., Clark, S., Soutter, M., Johannsen, J., & Malhotra, S. (2020, December 10). Critical consciousness: A key to student achievement. kappanonline.org. Retrieved December 23, 2021, from https://kappanonline.org/critical-consciousness-key-student-achievement/

Farmer, G. (2021, April 19). How schools and teachers can get better at Cultural Competence. Education Next. Retrieved December 23, 2021, from https://www.educationnext.org/how-schools-teachers-can-get-better-cultural-competence/

Ferlazzo, L. (2021, July 13). Author interview with dr. Gholdy Muhammad: 'Cultivating genius' (opinion). Education Week. Retrieved December 23, 2021, from https://www.edweek.org/teaching-learning/opinion-author-interview-with-dr-gholdy-muhammad-cultivating-genius/2020/01

Finley, T., & Wiggs, B. (2016). Rethinking classroom design: Create student-centered learning spaces for 6th-12th graders. Rowman & Littlefield.

Garner, B. (2008, March 1). When students seem stalled. ASCD. Retrieved December 28, 2021, from https://www.ascd.org/el/articles/when-students-seem-stalled

Hammond, Z., & Jackson, Y. (2015). Culturally responsive teaching and the brain: Promoting authentic engagement and rigor among culturally and linguistically diverse students. Corwin.

Harchegani, A., & Ishihara-Wing, G. (n.d.). Analyzing Groupwork Videos & Developing Group Norms . Retrieved December 23, 2021, from https://docs.google.com/document/d/14iEYFO9tL3OrDqRXcYzjXD9goPd0MiRNFIHTofzVjXU/edit#heading=h.3dy6vkm

Harp, R. (2021, November 15). MediaINDIGENA. Retrieved December 30, 2021, from https://mediaindigena.com/

Hong, J. (2021, February 17). *Black students still more likely to face harsh discipline.* KPBS. https://www.kpbs.org/news/education/2021/02/17/study-black-students-still-more-likely-face-harsh

Horton, M., & Freire, P. (1990). *We make the road by walking: Conversations on education and social change.* Temple Univ. Pr.

Kokozos, M., & Gonzalez, M. (2021, February 15). Cultivating critical consciousness in the classroom: 10 Counternarrative Resources. Getting Smart. Retrieved December 23, 2021, from https://www.gettingsmart.com/2021/02/15/cultivating-critical-consciousness-in-the-classroom-ten-counternarrative-resources/

Liberated spaces: Purposeful school design says goodbye to cells and Bells. EdCan Network. (2012, November 8). Retrieved December 23, 2021, from https://www.edcan.ca/articles/liberated-spaces-purposeful-school-design-says-goodbye-to-cells-and-bells/

Lim, D. (2020, November 8). Qualities of regenerative and liberating culture. Medium Retrieved December 26, 2021, from https://regenerative.medium.com/qualities-of-regenerative-and-liberating-culture-9d3809b30557

Love, B. L. (2019). *We want to do more than survive: abolitionist teaching and the pursuit of educational freedom.* Boston, Massachusetts: Beacon Press.

Marentette, L. (2017, October 17). Characteristics of innovative learning spaces that you should know. Collaborative software solutions. Retrieved December 23, 2021, from https://www.nuiteq.com/company/blog/characteristics-of-innovative-learning-spaces-that-you-should-know

Milvidskaia, Y., Tebelman, T., & Hsu, L. (n.d.). Rolling Out Group Roles. Retrieved December 23, 2021, from https://docs.google.com/document/d/1-SA4eIG4oeQ_XPcy51ORVWEkHSb-5FzayLQZBmIuAdU/edit#heading=h.3dy6vkm

Moon, T. R. (2011). Projectimplicit. Take a Test. Retrieved December 23, 2021, from https://implicit.harvard.edu/implicit/takeatest.html

Muhammad, G. (2021). Cultivating genius: An equity framework for culturally and historically responsive literacy. Scholastic.

My Cultura Podcasts. iHeart. (n.d.). Retrieved December 30, 2021, from https://www.iheart.com/podcast/1299-my-cultura-podcasts-86658576/

National Association of Independent Schools. (2018, June 22). *Kimberlé Crenshaw: What is intersectionality* [video]. YouTube. https://www.youtube.com/watch?v=ViDtnfQ9FHc

National Center for Restorative Justice. (n.d.). Retrieved December 23, 2021, from https://www.nationalcenterforrestorativejustice.com/

National Equity Project. (n.d.). Academic mindsets - scoe. Excerpts from Farrington, C.A., Roderick, M., Allensworth, E., Nagaoka, J., Keyes, T.S., Johnson, D.W., & Beechum, N.O. (2012). Teaching adolescents to become learners. The role of noncognitive factors in shaping school performance: A critical literature review. Chicago: University of Chicago Consortium on Chicago School Research. Retrieved December 23, 2021, from https://www.scoe.org/blog_files/Academic%20Mindsets.pdf

Patton, A. (Ed.). (2021, October 1). Project Card Home. High Tech High Unboxed. Retrieved December 28, 2021, from https://hthunboxed.org/project-card-home/

Peoples, D'Andrea Martínez, & Foster. (2020). Knowing Young People in 4 Dimensions Empathy Interview. Retrieved December 23, 2021, from https://docs.google.com/document/d/1WHungw3icYqKsW6J2_cHyTfbZaI6yHvOrmy3W0KQyiQ/edit

Pledger, M. S. (2008). Backwards Design Template. Retrieved December 23, 2021, from https://docs.google.com/document/d/1lTGC_QCLlI2I-c9h9c8L8jCmvCyPJMo2WYIIxWqxnQ/edit

Pledger, M. S. (2018). *Cultivating Culturally Responsive Reform: The Intersectionality of Backgrounds and Beliefs on Culturally Responsive Teaching Behaviors.* University of California, San Diego.

Ramos-Brannon, I., & Muhammed, G. (2020, May 20). Teaching toward genius: an equity model for pedagogy in action. Equity & Access Pre K-12 | The American Consortium for Equity in Education. Retrieved December 26, 2021, from https://ace-ed.org/teaching-toward-genius-an-equity-model-for-pedagogy-in-action/

Resources · science in the city. Science in the City. (2021). Retrieved December 26, 2021, from https://scienceinthecity.stanford.edu/resources/

Seale, C. (2018, September 18). When love is grounded in the soft bigotry of low expectations, it's the wrong kind of Love. Education Post. Retrieved December 28, 2021, from https://educationpost.org/when-love-is-grounded-in-the-soft-bigotry-of-low-expectations-its-the-wrong-kind-of-love/

Seven CS for Effective Teaching ASCD. (2016, September 1). Retrieved December 23, 2021, from https://www.ascd.org/el/articles/seven-cs-for-effective-teachingSingleton, G. E. (2022). *Courageous conversations about race: A field guide for achieving equity in schools and beyond.* Corwin.

Smith, K. (2020, September 24). Cultivating critical consciousness in the classroom. Facing Today - A Facing History Blog. Retrieved December 23, 2021, from https://facingtoday.facinghistory.org/cultivating-critical-consciousness-in-the-classroom

Social Justice Math in action: From educational model to educational movement. Just Equations. (2020, November 20). Retrieved December 26, 2021, from https://justequations.org/resource/social-justice-math-in-action-webinar/

Sriram, R. (2020, April 13). The neuroscience behind productive struggle. Edutopia. Retrieved December 28, 2021, from https://www.edutopia.org/article/neuroscience-behind-productive-struggle

Story Corps. (2012). Facundo the Great. Retrieved December 23, 2021, from https://www.youtube.com/watch?v=s8FheuSE7w4.

Style, E. (2016). Curriculum as Window and Mirror. Social Science Record, Fall. https://doi.org/https://nationalseedproject.org/images/documents/Curriculum_As_Window_and_Mirror.pdf

Style, E. J. (2014). Curriculum as Encounter: Selves and Shelves . English Journal, 103(5), 67–74. https://doi.org/https://nationalseedproject.org/images/documents/Curriculum_as_Encounter.pdf

Tara J. Yosso (2005) Whose culture has capital? A critical race theory discussion of community cultural wealth, Race Ethnicity and Education, 8:1, 69-91, DOI: 10.1080/1361332052000341006

Teaching materials archive. Zinn Education Project. (2021). Retrieved December 28, 2021, from https://www.zinnedproject.org/materials/

TedTalks. (2016). The Urgency of Intersectionality. Youtube. Retrieved December 27, 2021, from https://www.youtube.com/watch?v=akOe5-UsQ2o.

TedXBrandeis University. (n.d.). Say Less: A Lesson in Code Switching. Say Less. Retrieved December 25, 2021, from https://www.ted.com/talks/naya_stevens_say_less_a_lesson_in_code_switching.

TEDxMaysHighSchool. (2018). To Code Switch or not to Code Switch. Youtube. Retrieved December 27, 2021, from https://www.youtube.com/watch?v=sncGGjaYJ5I.

TedXMcMinnville. (2019). Getting it right; why pronouncing names correctly matters. Ted. Retrieved December 23, 2021, from https://www.ted.com/talks/gerardo_ochoa_getting_it_right_why_pronouncing_names_correctly_matters.Terrell, R. D., Terrell, E. K., Lindsey, R. B., Lindsey, D. B., & Alpert, D. (2018). *Culturally proficient leadership: The personal journey begins within.* Corwin, a SAGE Publishing Company.

Various definitions under chapter titles. (n.d.). In *New Oxford American dictionary* (Second Edition). Retrieved from personal Mac computer built-in software.

Youtube. (2015). The Learning Pit. Retrieved December 25, 2021, from https://www.youtube.com/watch?v=3IMUAOhuO78.

Recommended Reading List

Books Related to Self Work
- *Culturally Proficient Leadership*
- *Eloquent Rage*
- *For Brown Girls with Sharp Edges and Tender Hearts*
- *So You Wanna Talk About Race*
- *I'm Still Here: Black Dignity in a World Made for Whiteness*
- *White Fragility*
- *Impact with Integrity: Repair the World Without Breaking Yourself*

Books Related to Organizational Development and/or Coaching
- *Courageous Conversations about Race*
- *Shattering Inequities*
- *The Listening Leader*
- *Coaching for Equity*
- *Street Data*
- *The Art of Coaching Teams*
- *Grading for Equity*
- *The Make or Break Year*

Books Related to Culturally Responsive Pedagogy/Abolitionist Teaching
- *Other People's Children: Culture Conflict in the Classroom*
- *Multiplication is for White People: Raising Expectations for Other People's Children*
- *The Dreamkeepers: Successful Teachers of African Americans*

- *Culturally Responsive Teaching: Theory, Research and Practice*
- *Culturally Responsive Teaching and the Brain*
- *Cultivating Genius*
- *Culturally Sustaining Pedagogies*
- *We Got This*
- *We Want to do More than Survive*
- *For White Folks Who Teach in the Hood*
- *Ratchedemic*

Contributor Biographies

Michelle Sadrena Pledger, Ed.D., Author

Michelle Sadrena Pledger is the Director of Liberation at the Center for Research on Equity and Innovation, a center that brings together practitioners, researchers and youth to address complex problems of practice in K-12 education and create more equitable, engaging learning environments for all young people. As a faculty member at High Tech High's Graduate School of Education, she teaches "Justice: Self, Schools, and Society", "Leadership for School Change", and "Culturally Responsive Continuous Improvement". Michelle also works as a Freedom Facilitator and consults with organizations and districts who seek to liberate self, others, and systems. She is committed to disrupting inequity in education and cultivating a community of practitioners who honor the lived experiences of all their young people and educators. Whether it is through the vehicle of project based learning, culturally responsive-sustaining pedagogy, or freedom facilitation, Michelle's hope is to develop educators and young people who think critically, act empathetically, and live for liberation.

Aisha Bain, Foreword

Aisha is the Co-Founder and Chief Architect of Resistance Communications, a creative action agency that works with local power to elevate the voices and visibility of women, girls, youth and resistors fighting for social justice through radical storytelling, transformative programming, and art grounded in strategy for social change. As a filmmaker, artist and author, Aisha has a particular passion for using creative tools and media to further social justice movements, and to raise the voice and visibility of women and girls within those movements. Through her work, Aisha facilitates the internal healing and visionary development of organizations and individuals, and uses her insurgent imagination to collaboratively design programs, develop models for action, creatively problem solving and deepening community strength, movement building and transformation.

Krista Galleberg, Editor

Krista Galleberg is a fifth grade teacher at High Tech Elementary Chula Vista, a project-based learning school in Chula Vista, CA. Krista loves to design innovative projects in partnership with linguistically and culturally diverse learners and their families. In addition to classroom teaching, Krista has served as a member of the founding team for a diverse by design elementary school in Saint Louis, MO and has worked with education researchers to write about the future of education. Krista is passionate about contributing to schools that interrupt patterns of white supremacy and other forms of inequality to create a more equal and democratic society. When she is not teaching, researching or writing, Krista loves to spend time outdoors or with her family.

CHIKLE, Cover Artist and In-Text Illustrator

Enrique Lugo, aka Chikle, is the proud son of Mexican Immigrants. He is a cultural worker dedicated to progressive education and community activism. His work as an Arts Educator is centered around identity, cultivating safe spaces and a sense of belonging for all. Passionate about commUNITY, Enrique continues to be involved in activism, promoting entrepreneurship, producing family friendly events, and curating art shows.

Made in the USA
Middletown, DE
20 May 2024